Belle City Gifts
Savage, Minnesota, USA

Belle City Gifts is an imprint of BroadStreet Publishing Group LLC.
Broadstreetpublishing.com

CORAL FLORAL Pocket Planner
© 2018 by BroadStreet Publishing ®

ISBN 978-1-4245-5707-3

All Scripture has been taken from The Passion Translation® of the Holy Bible. Copyright © 2014, 2015 by BroadStreet Publishing. All rights reserved.

Design by Chris Garborg | garborgdesign.com
Compiled and edited by Michelle Winger | literallyprecise.com

Printed in China.

JANUARY
2019

WE DON'T SEE OURSELVES AS CAPABLE ENOUGH TO DO ANYTHING IN OUR OWN STRENGTH, FOR OUR TRUE COMPETENCE FLOWS FROM GOD'S EMPOWERING PRESENCE.

2 CORINTHIANS 3:5

SUNDAY	MONDAY	TUESDAY	WEDNESDAY	THURSDAY	FRIDAY	SATURDAY
		1 New Year's Day	2	3	4	5
6	7	8	9	10	11	12

13	14	15	16	17	18	19
20	21 Martin Luther King Jr. Day	22	23	24	25	26
27	28	29	30	31		

FEBRUARY
2019

"My grace is always more than enough for you, and my power finds its full expression in your weakness."

2 CORINTHIANS 12:9

SUNDAY	MONDAY	TUESDAY	WEDNESDAY	THURSDAY	FRIDAY	SATURDAY
					1	2
3	4	5	6	7	8	9
13	14	15	16	17	18	19
20	21 Winter Solstice	22	23	24 Christmas Eve	25 Christmas Day	26
27	28	29	30	31 New Year's Eve		

DECEMBER
2020

SUNDAY	MONDAY	TUESDAY	WEDNESDAY	THURSDAY	FRIDAY	SATURDAY
		1	2	3	4	5
6	7	8	9	10 Hanukkah begins	11	12
10	11	12	13	14 Valentine's Day	15	16
17	18 President's Day	19	20	21	22	23
24	25	26	27	28		

MARCH 2019

"DON'T WORRY OR SURRENDER TO YOUR FEAR. FOR IF YOU'VE BELIEVED IN GOD, NOW TRUST AND BELIEVE IN ME ALSO."

JOHN 14:1

SUNDAY	MONDAY	TUESDAY	WEDNESDAY	THURSDAY	FRIDAY	SATURDAY
					1	2
3	4	5	6 Ash Wednesday	7	8	9
15	16	17	18	19	20	21
22	23	24	25	26 Thanksgiving Day	27	28
29 First Sunday of Advent	30					

November 2020

SUNDAY	MONDAY	TUESDAY	WEDNESDAY	THURSDAY	FRIDAY	SATURDAY
1 Daylight Saving Time ends	2	3	4	5	6	7
8	9	10	11 Veterans' Day	12	13	14
10 Daylight Saving Time begins	11	12	13	14	15	16
17 St. Patrick's Day	18	19	20 Spring Equinox	21	22	23
24	25	26	27	28	29	30
31						

APRIL
2019

POUR OUT ALL YOUR WORRIES AND STRESS UPON HIM AND LEAVE THEM THERE, FOR HE ALWAYS TENDERLY CARES FOR YOU.

1 PETER 5:7

SUNDAY	MONDAY	TUESDAY	WEDNESDAY	THURSDAY	FRIDAY	SATURDAY
	1	2	3	4	5	6
7	8	9	10	11	12	13
11	12 Columbus Day	13	14	15	16	17
18	19	20	21	22	23	24
25	26	27	28	29	30	31

OCTOBER
2020

SUNDAY	MONDAY	TUESDAY	WEDNESDAY	THURSDAY	FRIDAY	SATURDAY
				1	2	3
4	5	6	7	8	9	10
14 Palm Sunday	15	16	17	18	19 Good Friday	20 First Day of Passover
21 Easter Sunday	22	23	24	25	26	27 Last Day of Passover
28	29	30				

MAY 2019

EVERYTHING WE COULD EVER NEED FOR LIFE AND COMPLETE DEVOTION TO GOD HAS ALREADY BEEN DEPOSITED IN US BY HIS DIVINE POWER.

2 PETER 1:3

SUNDAY	MONDAY	TUESDAY	WEDNESDAY	THURSDAY	FRIDAY	SATURDAY
			1	2 National Day of Prayer	3	4
5	6	7	8	9	10	11
13	14	15	16	17	18	19 Rosh Hashanah
20	21	22 Autumnal Equinox	23	24	25	26
27 Yom Kippur	28	29	30			

SEPTEMBER
2020

SUNDAY	MONDAY	TUESDAY	WEDNESDAY	THURSDAY	FRIDAY	SATURDAY
		1	2	3	4	5
6	7 Labor Day	8	9	10	11	12
12 Mother's Day	13	14	15	16	17	18
19	20	21	22	23	24	25
26	27 Memorial Day	28	29	30	31	

JUNE 2019

SINCE WE HAVE THIS CONFIDENCE, WE CAN ALSO HAVE GREAT BOLDNESS BEFORE HIM, FOR IF WE PRESENT ANY REQUEST AGREEABLE TO HIS WILL, HE WILL HEAR US.

1 JOHN 5:14

SUNDAY	MONDAY	TUESDAY	WEDNESDAY	THURSDAY	FRIDAY	SATURDAY
						1
2	3	4	5	6	7	8
9	10	11	12	13	14	15
16	17	18	19	20	21	22
23	24	25	26	27	28	29
30	31					

AUGUST
2020

SUNDAY	MONDAY	TUESDAY	WEDNESDAY	THURSDAY	FRIDAY	SATURDAY
						1
2	3	4	5	6	7	8
9 Pentecost	10	11	12	13	14	15
16 Father's Day	17	18	19	20	21 Summer Solstice	22
23	24	25	26	27	28	29
30						

JULY 2019

CHEER UP! TAKE COURAGE ALL YOU WHO LOVE HIM.
WAIT FOR HIM TO BREAK THROUGH FOR YOU, ALL WHO TRUST IN HIM!

PSALM 31:24

SUNDAY	MONDAY	TUESDAY	WEDNESDAY	THURSDAY	FRIDAY	SATURDAY
	1	2	3	4 Independence Day	5	6
7	8	9	10	11	12	13
12	13	14	15	16	17	18
19	20	21	22	23	24	25
26	27	28	29	30	31	

JULY
2020

SUNDAY	MONDAY	TUESDAY	WEDNESDAY	THURSDAY	FRIDAY	SATURDAY
			1	2	3	4 Independence Day
5	6	7	8	9	10	11
14	15	16	17	18	19	20
21	22	23	24	25	26	27
28	29	30	31			

AUGUST
2019

We constantly pray that our God will empower you to live worthy of all that he has invited you to experience.

2 THESSALONIANS 1:11

SUNDAY	MONDAY	TUESDAY	WEDNESDAY	THURSDAY	FRIDAY	SATURDAY
				1	2	3
4	5	6	7	8	9	10
14	15	16	17	18	19	20 Summer Solstice
21 Father's Day	22	23	24	25	26	27
28	29	30				

JUNE
2020

SUNDAY	MONDAY	TUESDAY	WEDNESDAY	THURSDAY	FRIDAY	SATURDAY
	1	2	3	4	5	6
7	8	9	10	11	12	13
11	12	13	14	15	16	17
18	19	20	21	22	23	24
25	26	27	28	29	30	31

SEPTEMBER
2019

BRILLIANT IDEAS PAY OFF AND BRING YOU PROSPERITY,
BUT MAKING HASTY, IMPATIENT DECISIONS WILL ONLY
LEAD TO FINANCIAL LOSS.

PROVERBS 21:5

SUNDAY	MONDAY	TUESDAY	WEDNESDAY	THURSDAY	FRIDAY	SATURDAY
1	2 Labor Day	3	4	5	6	7
8	9	10	11	12	13	14
10 Mother's Day	11	12	13	14	15	16
17	18	19	20	21	22	23
24	25 Memorial Day	26	27	28	29	30
31 Pentecost						

MAY
2020

SUNDAY	MONDAY	TUESDAY	WEDNESDAY	THURSDAY	FRIDAY	SATURDAY
					1	2
3	4	5	6	7 National Day of Prayer	8	9
15	16	17	18	19	20	21
22	23 Autumnal Equinox	24	25	26	27	28
29	30 Rosh Hashanah					

OCTOBER 2019

Put your heart and soul into every activity you do, as though you are doing it for the Lord himself and not merely for others.

COLOSSIANS 3:23

SUNDAY	MONDAY	TUESDAY	WEDNESDAY	THURSDAY	FRIDAY	SATURDAY
		1	2	3	4	5
6	7	8 Yom Kippur	9	10	11	12
12 Easter Sunday	13	14	15	16 Last Day of Passover	17	18
19	20	21	22	23	24	25
26	27	28	29	30		

APRIL
2020

SUNDAY	MONDAY	TUESDAY	WEDNESDAY	THURSDAY	FRIDAY	SATURDAY
			1	2	3	4
5 Palm Sunday	6	7	8 First Day of Passover	9	10 Good Friday	11
13	14 Columbus Day	15	16	17	18	19
20	21	22	23	24	25	26
27	28	29	30	31		

NOVEMBER 2019

DISCOVER CREATIVE WAYS TO ENCOURAGE OTHERS AND TO MOTIVATE THEM TOWARD ACTS OF COMPASSION, DOING BEAUTIFUL WORKS AS EXPRESSIONS OF LOVE.

HEBREWS 10:24

SUNDAY	MONDAY	TUESDAY	WEDNESDAY	THURSDAY	FRIDAY	SATURDAY
					1	2
3 Daylight Saving Time ends	4	5	6	7	8	9
15	16	17 St. Patrick's Day	18	19	20 Spring Equinox	21
22	23	24	25	26	27	28
29	30	31				

MARCH
2020

SUNDAY	MONDAY	TUESDAY	WEDNESDAY	THURSDAY	FRIDAY	SATURDAY
1	2	3	4	5	6	7
8 Daylight Saving Time begins	9	10	11	12	13	14
10	11 Veterans' Day	12	13	14	15	16
17	18	19	20	21	22	23
24	25	26	27	28 Thanksgiving Day	29	30

DECEMBER

2019

WHEN WE LIVE OUR LIVES WITHIN THE SHADOW OF THE GOD MOST HIGH, OUR SECRET HIDING PLACE, WE WILL ALWAYS BE SHIELDED FROM HARM.

PSALM 91:9

SUNDAY	MONDAY	TUESDAY	WEDNESDAY	THURSDAY	FRIDAY	SATURDAY
1 First Sunday of Advent	2	3	4	5	6	7
8	9	10	11	12	13	14
9	10	11	12	13	14 Valentine's Day	15
16	17 President's Day	18	19	20	21	22
23	24	25	26 Ash Wednesday	27	28	29

FEBRUARY
2020

SUNDAY	MONDAY	TUESDAY	WEDNESDAY	THURSDAY	FRIDAY	SATURDAY
						1
2	3	4	5	6	7	8
15	16	17	18	19	20	21
22 Winter Solstice	23 Hanukkah begins	24 Christmas Eve	25 Christmas Day	26	27	28
29	30 Hanukkah ends	31 New Year's Eve				

JANUARY
2020

WITHIN YOUR HEART YOU CAN MAKE PLANS FOR YOUR FUTURE,
BUT THE LORD CHOOSES THE STEPS YOU TAKE TO GET THERE.

PROVERBS 16:9

SUNDAY	MONDAY	TUESDAY	WEDNESDAY	THURSDAY	FRIDAY	SATURDAY
			1 New Year's Day	2	3	4
5	6	7	8	9	10	11
12	13	14	15	16	17	18
19	20 Martin Luther King Jr. Day	21	22	23	24	25
26	27	28	29	30	31	